Transit Authority

Also by

TONY SANDERS

Partial Eclipse

TRANSIT AUTHORITY

Poems

TONY SANDERS

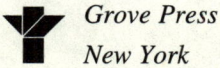 Grove Press
New York

Published simultaneously in Canada
Printed in the United States of America

FIRST EDITION

Library of Congress Cataloging-in-Publication Data
Sanders, Tony, 1957–
   Transit authority : poems / by Tony Sanders.
     p. cm.
   ISBN 0-8021-3677-X
    I. Title.
   PS3569.A51385 T73 2000
   811'.54—dc21   99-052856

Design by Julie Duquet

Grove Press
841 Broadway
New York, NY 10003

00 01 02 03 10 9 8 7 6 5 4 3 2 1

I would like to thank Richard Howard for his unflagging encouragement and support. I would also like to express my gratitude to Chard deNiord, Janet Krauss, David Lazar, and Robert Zaretsky. This book is dedicated to Matthew, Jack, and, especially, Linda.

ACKNOWLEDGMENTS

Many thanks to the editors of the publications in which the following poems have appeared or will soon appear: *Alembic*: "Winter Borough," "The Shore"; *Confrontation*: "Hell Gate Bridge"; *The Gettysburg Review*: "West Street"; *Green Mountains Review*: "Wild Momentum," "Post-Achillean"; *Gulf Coast*: "Late Watch," excerpts from "Street Music"; *The Ohio Review*: "Psalm"; *The Paris Review*: "Between Wars," "Exchange Place," "Trinity at Noon," "Fulton and Pearl," "Minetta Street, Nos. 2, 4, 6: 1935," "Peerless Equipment Co.," "Montaigne," "Late Victorian," "Counting Down," "Locomotive"; *The Yale Review*: "Transit Authority"; *Western Humanities Review*: "Self Service," "One Part," "Westerly," "Summer Reading," "On Religion"; "Transit Authority" also appeared in *Best American Poetry 1995*

CONTENTS

MONTAIGNE *1*

I: BETWEEN WARS *3*

LATE WATCH *5*
COUNTING DOWN *6*
SUMMER READING *7*
LATE VICTORIAN *9*
TERMINAL *11*
BETWEEN WARS *12*
TWO POEMS BEGINNING WITH WORDS FROM STENDHAL *15*
WINTER BOROUGH *17*

II: WEST STREET *21*

HELL GATE BRIDGE *23*
FULTON AND PEARL *24*
TRINITY AT NOON *25*
TRAVELING TIN SHOP *26*
EXCHANGE PLACE *27*
CHURCH AND STATE *28*
WASHINGTON SQUARE, LOOKING NORTH *29*

Court of the First Model Tenements (I) 30
Court of the First Model Tenements (II) 31
Peerless Equipment Co. 32
Henry Street 33
Old-Law Tenements: First Street 34
Minetta Street Nos. 2, 4, 6: 1935 35
West Street 36

III: Reckoning 39

The Shore 41
Recreational 44
Westerly 45
Wild Momentum 48
Locomotive 50
Self Service 51
One Part 52
On Religion 53
Psalm 54
Night Commute 55
Serial 58
Post-Achillean 59
Street Music 61
Transit Authority 66
Reckoning 68

Transit Authority

MONTAIGNE

I hate bow ties. Allow me to digress.
Remember that leafy aphorisms
sometimes grow out of idle burbling
and look different when they're not in season.
What Horace calls "bumptious candor" exists
in each crop of an essayist's half-truths.
Imagine me standing in the mirror,
an airplane's idle prop around my neck.
What color should mine be? A red clip-on?
Something to divert the crowd from my eyes
might come in handy when I contradict
myself. Clothing is vocabulary;
the body is nothing more than grammar.
I would wear anything, even breeches.

I

I

Between Wars

LATE WATCH

The end of the century overstimulates itself to such an extent that clouds wamble off at half-mast

only to reappear in white ties and tails to be the life of the party on the dizzy horizon past midnight.

And there are others in a tipsy mode despite the fact that nature is out back polishing the gangplank.

Even if we could find the home number of someone with a reputation for navigation in such waters

we'd be destined to get a busy signal or voice mail or at the very best get put on hold forever.

Too bad we aren't on board with someone at the tiller who barks *steady as she goes* and means it,

but by the time another day's sun slumps under the yardarm our situation continues its listing.

Maybe we should consider abandoning ship except that the majority of the lifeboats are snoring,

even though the mainsail makes an infernal luffing and somewhere a halyard pulley whacks metal.

Maybe we should consider why the gulls that followed the boat from the beginning aren't circling.

Counting Down

It was as though the very day itself were wearing a see-through blouse weeks before
a mastectomy,
something in the air wanting desperately to draw attention to itself if only to assuage
awkwardness
by forcing itself to face up to the fact that nature's penchant for symmetry could not
continue,
but nobody stopped watching the electric numbers blinking above the double doors
floor by floor,
nobody dared utter a word in the silence that seemed related to the indistinct lighting
on the ceiling,
not because there was something sacred about the way they were drifting earthward
from on high,
where if they wanted they could have had a panoramic view of a city of late stricken
with a fever,
where they could have waited until gradually darkness itself filtered into the evening
like disease
simultaneously working its way toward the surface as well as the center of the body
close to death,
but because they were so uncertain of what would become of them they had nothing
right to say.

SUMMER READING

Everyone has the same books.
        The problem is the ideas have packed up
and fled to Connecticut for the weekend,
        meaning that there's a torpor in the air.
The awnings must be aware of it
        the way they hang limply over the fruit,
the taxis too with broad yellow hoods
        cracked slightly open as if gasping for air.

You get the idea that if it were, say, fall,
        the pay phone on the corner might ring
at just the moment when you pass by,
        but there's been a run on little miracles,
nobody knows when the next order's due.
        Encouraging signs are only momentary:
the white cotton bedsheet hung out to dry
        on a line stretching between two fire escapes

billows as if it were the wind-filled spinnaker
        of a famous ship at sea until reality settles in,
the laundry resuming its habit of drying out.

Meanwhile, the real wind is persistent
as it ruffles the dust jacket of a great epic
    resting on the sand by the plastic cooler
while someone grown bored with the plot
    walks to the lighthouse and back, or wades in.

LATE VICTORIAN

The early days subscribed to us,
       first warming to our blandishments,
but we, having practiced praise
       in front of mirrors facing mirrors
and knowing how to give as well as
       to take no for an answer, retreated.

It's not as if we backed out
       of the parlor like a damaged widower
looking mournfully at the baby grand
       now forever silent in the alcove,
it's not as if we took one last look
       at the sober portrait above the mantel.

Of course, we never left the premises,
       only moved to a room with less finery,
where, had we wanted, we could have sat
       and looked out of a dormer and wondered
what we had done to let the starch
       run out of the landscape.

. . .

Maybe we never had the stomach
                for the brocade world we created
or, rather, had made in the Far East
                and shipped halfway round the world,
so that even on the sunniest of summer days
                we could keep out the light,

though light was what we were,
                at least on the surface, always rising
to the occasion like an infinity
                of miniature champagne bubbles in a flute,
while in our hearts what we wanted to do
                was hurl the glass into the fire.

TERMINAL

How much longer can time go on twiddling its thumbs as it sits in the waiting room
of a bus depot
not far from the terminal lunch counter where two cascades of grape punch splash
in perpetuity,
while the hot dogs turn clockwise, some blistered and charred, some just beginning
to sweat,
by coincidence on the busiest night of the year because every so often it wants to be
with strangers
all bundled up and laden down with shopping bags of boxes wrapped and ribboned
for family,
until one by one, or often in groups of two or three under the bare light, they shuffle
out of sight
only to be replaced by more travelers, who stare in anticipation at the ceiling speaker
for a voice
grown so familiar with the notion of hours and minutes it is now completely devoid
of tone
to bark out arrivals and departures long into the night until at some point everybody
is en route,
be it a twenty-minute ride to relatives on the outskirts of the city or a five-day mecca
back home.

II

Between Wars

What else is there to do but watch carefully for any noticeable movement by a statue of a past hero,
the great arm of general so-and-so astride his steed not far from the hot-dog vendors and carriages
raised to make a point long after the company has packed up and ridden double-time into history.
Epaulets are popular among the legions pacing on both sides of the militarized zone of day traffic,
as are army boots and bayonet necklaces and an occasional pair of designer fatigues lined with fur.
Even a weather-beaten crone gets in on the act by throwing salvos of bread crumbs at dense circles
of pigeons momentarily detonated by each round of manna until they finally resume their feeding.

All the buildings along the avenue stand at attention as if waiting for a past president to drive by
at the moment all the uppermost windows might open and let go a sky full of confetti and banners.
But nothing monumental really happens. Traffic floats by like tires and metal drums in a flood,

past trees that maintain a leafy indifference in spite of trunks that bear flesh wounds
from exhaust,
past squadrons of see-me-nots haranguing crowds of passersby waiting impatiently
at a bus stop,
while, above, barely detectable ribbons of clouds race by in a kind of controlled panic
of liberation,
as when something goes awry in the subway and the passengers file out one by one
like prisoners.

Something in the air smacks of desperate measures being mulled over in the secrecy
of back rooms,
the kind with rows of different-colored telephones and wall maps of a city twinkling
like tree lights.
Rumor has it some decision will be arrived at shortly, so the only thing to do is wait
as the hours
march by in minutes as cold and efficient as recruits just discharged with distinction
from boot camp.
People examine the sky with the expressions of those who suspect the air-raid siren
is broken,
though the only thing that seems out of place is the blimp floating precariously close
to buildings,
as though under orders to take these measures needed to wrap up its reconnaissance
and head home.
. . .

It's eerie to live in an age when ordinary people look like they've just received word
from the front.

Everyone is tuned to an imaginary broadcast in order to find out what has happened
to the next of kin,

but the reporter who speaks of shrapnel and the mounting casualties cannot give out
names of dead,

so there is nothing to do but get on with the business of daily life, which now seems
like maneuvers.

And yet, no day passes without the need to look up at the eyes of an embossed hero
for reassurance,

some glint of relief in a face remarkably unsullied despite the fact it is frozen forever
in mid-battle,

because there's still a part of us that imagines the inevitable outcome will be victory,
even Pyrrhic.

Two Poems Beginning with Words from Stendhal

I

"Perhaps men who cannot love passionately are those who feel the effects of beauty most keenly."

Meaning a loner stands on the other side of a storefront window as the mannequins stare ahead

with the androgynous vacuity of models who have been refining the perfect postures all their lives.

A butt that has been flicked to the gutter and the parabolic arc it makes before hitting back water

with a hiss that's murdered by silence is often all to know of the unspoken narrative gone awry.

A crowded ferry backing out of the harbor bound for Liberty or Ellis islands lets go an oil slick

that negotiates the swells and sloughs of the river like some rare aquatic invertebrate from the past,

if only for a moment before it begins the innate process of division and subdivision into nothing

but the eerie sheen someone alone leaning over the aft rail mulling over his love life might notice

and think it analogous to the latest shimmering romance that's been pulled sideways
into the wake.

II

"I'm constantly beset by the fear I may have expressed a sigh when I thought I was
stating a truth"
is what anybody might say in confidence to a friend when the subject of pure desire
resurfaces,
as if at dark moments in adulthood there's the revelation that the heart is sequestered
from the mind
in solitary confinement, so that the sole indication of the other is the turning of pages
in the next cell.
But the emaciated light disguised as the sun seeping into the asymmetrical windows
of the skull
is enough to put the the old picture-making process in motion even before the coffee
and hard roll,
another morning to survey the shadows on the wall that have come to be so familiar
around dawn,
when the only philosophy is the philosophy of brooms sweeping grit from the curb
down below.
This is the missing hour when there is so little to dwell on that mere air is the source
for reflection,
as though fortified by the long night it goes in and out of the body of its own accord
for love.

WINTER BOROUGH

The days of mutual admiration come and go
        and come again replete with fulsome asides
so that everybody looks more than numinous
        in a kind of electric, Christmas-ornament way.

Just as holidays give way to a mass nutation,
        so they snap to with a start at a dropped fork
or a flute tapped to clear the air for the toast.
        Sometimes it feels as if uniformed members

of a parade band are gathering in the distance
        where blue barricades are up to tame a crowd,
but the trouble with such a laudable inkling is
        the way the streets are afterward when brooms

push paper and, once in a while, a child's glove.
        There must be some kind of allegory in play,
but that sort of thing's dropped out of fashion
        and sits nodding out at home, dreaming of return.

. . .

There are those hell-bent on waxing nostalgic
        who must be treated with a modicum of grace,
given that their condition is always progressive.
        Remember that for them there's no way back.

But not to dwell on the negative, the grand idea
        of the marching band high-stepping up the avenue
again surges to the forefront of consciousness
        like a kid needling past adults to see the parade.

Meanwhile the streets simply wait to be mended
        by a change in weather, another mood sidling in
from the west with the promise of crafty lather
        to take from view the presence of hard edges.

To think: far off a simoom spreads its breath
        over the monslike dunes of the Arabian desert
and gradually the terrain turns into a close relative
        of its former self albeit recognizable to Bedouins.

And yet, there's no need for the bank of TVs
        tuned to the weather channel in the store window
making the planet look like a hi-tech brain scan
        of a patient just diagnosed with a malignant tumor.

. . .

The feeling "we're all in this together" comes
                and goes like packs of taxis roaming "off-duty"
through neighborhoods with cinder buildings
                now too tired-looking to have any personality.

Even holidays have lost much of their sheen;
                the pennants are lengthening their frown lines
from being furled and unfurled so many times,
                the balloons barely holding out against slow leaks.

Mercifully, any side street leads to the water.
                There is still something restorative about the edge
of a river and its unceremonious procession,
                even if the weather has deteriorated into fine rain.

It has everything to do with the putting of hands
                on the railing to marvel at the river's insouciance.
But sometimes a moment of solitude has a halo
                that fades into the distance without waving goodbye.

II

WEST STREET

based on photographs by Berenice Abbott

HELL GATE BRIDGE

Funny how an entire era can be summed up by the parabolic arch of the steel bridge
over the river

when you stand on one shore near enough to be dwarfed by the structure extending
away from you,

how its intricate network of girders and spansions rises gracefully toward the center
like a cat

captured stretching after a nap or the superstructure of an enormous model dinosaur
in a museum.

Gradually you get the idea there is not much domestic or mechanical about two trees
with new leaves

in the foreground so close to the camera they are easy to overlook with the leviathan
in the distance,

nor the evanescent clouds overhead, both of which are in their way more determined
than we are.

FULTON AND PEARL

The rolled-up awning under the fire escape reads Hat Cleaning & Shoe Shine Parlor
in gray letters,
but the awning sags over the E and S of JOE's in the glass above a man alone inside
without a hat.
Joes Shoe & Ha Cleaning Parlor it says in letters with black borders in the window
without the man.
It says Joe's Shoe and Hat Cleaning in white letters in three rows on a cement pillar
next to the door.
A white straw hat painted on a thin pane about eye level reads in small print Cleaned
While You Wait.
Shoe Shine Parlor it says behind a feather duster by the daily newspapers and a box
of pale apples,
while a vendor stands in front of Joe's Shoe & Hat wearing a shabby change apron
and a clean hat.

TRINITY AT NOON

Although it is noon or roughly so, the church below is positioned like an hour hand
at eleven,
with its spire rising up in shadow as if the photographer wanted to relocate religions
in another time.
People on either side of the street at lunch hour run together like long lines of music
in a hymnal.
Nobody will ever know for sure why she chose the high floor she did to look down
on humanity,
or why she let the anonymous, dark windows of an office building across the street
be so dominant.
Nobody will ever know for sure why she chose the high floor she did to look down
on the cemetery
with the headstones facing forward like one might find in a cathedral barely half-full
at high mass.

TRAVELING TIN SHOP

The horse-drawn cart is so overladen it is initially hard to determine the organization
of the cookware
that the owner has stopped to secure at the curb of an uneven cobblestone side street
in Brooklyn
around midday, judging from the strength of the sun reflected in the metal saucepans
and the shadows
beneath the broad-bellied horse who seems unperturbed with his head pointed away
from the camera.
Gradually it becomes clear from the expression of the man whose eyes are protected
by a cap's brim,
and from the anonymous clapboard building in the background with all its windows
boarded up
and from wavy kettle stacks and blazing skillets dangling above him how few items
he ever sells.

Exchange Place

She could have clambered to the top of a skyscraper and photographed the sidewalk
at lunch hour
at a time when the narrow way would have been full of money men elbow to elbow
in blocked hats.
She could have stayed at street level and focused on the conspiracy of the buildings
to keep out sky,
so that few of the pedestrians ever took their eyes off newspapers or glanced higher
than wing tips.
It wasn't buildings or brokers in broadcloth that drew her to the far end of the street
several flights up,
nor was it an intricate cornice she wanted when she cropped most of the architecture
out of the picture.
It was how that long, slim corridor of commerce was designed to open only slightly
—like a new wallet.

CHURCH AND STATE

How could it be that a three-story building across from the Harlem Courthouse was
once a church?
Did all the now-anonymous worshipers sitting in narrow pews think about the law
yards away,
did they think about the piety of the jurors who sat through trial after trial out of duty
or drama,
as was the case with mothers who regarded a two-week jury summons as a reprieve
from children?
Did they think about how both the lawyers and the judge were in the habit of giving
pointed sermons
so that by the end of any given trial the responsibility of the jury with respect to fact
was minor?
How did the devout react when the church was renovated as a new law firm named
Flam & Flam?

Washington Square, Looking North

The thing about the stone arch that's been positioned in the center of the photograph
is its size,

not looming large in the foreground as one might expect a structure commemorating
Washington,

but set so far back it virtually recedes into the uniform row of brownstones dividing
earth and air.

The arch is nothing but a toy between those two titans, the broad-bellied skyscrapers
encroaching

upon an otherwise open and cloudless sky since it's still early enough in the century
to look up,

and a black-trunked tree to the left whose leafless right limb reaches across the park
ominously,

as if by some stretch of imagination it aims to obscure such progress in the distance
for a while.

Court of the First Model Tenements (I)

If there is anything even remotely human about an anonymous late-winter courtyard created

by a block of unpainted brick tenements with the salt that decades before has seeped to the surface,

it is the riot of laundry lines stretching from window after window to the wood pole in the center.

Unlike the maypole of yore or lore, the streamers festooning what must be close air in summer

sag under the burden of what comes in contact with the flesh of many difficult lives so often:

a row of seven bedsheets, for example, each sheet pinned in such a way it could be a nightgown

two or three urchins in the background might be scheming to pull down if it was not out of reach.

Court of the First Model Tenements (II)

The pole isn't much more than rough-hewn hardwood anchored in concrete poured
years ago

in a generally drab courtyard with walls turned inward to create a sense of too much
intimacy,

neverthless it is the long, black rip, the streak straight down the middle of the photo
that matters,

an imperfect axis tilting slightly to the right perhaps because of the pull of the cables
at the top,

maybe because of the lines of laundry sweeping out of the black windows on ropes
and pulleys,

the sheets and shirts and girdles and garters like pennants strung from a ship's mast
after a war,

though these are just the things people wear closest to their bodies in the clean years
before the war.

PEERLESS EQUIPMENT CO.

A man whose face is blurred sits with his feet on a barrel puffing a cigar and staring
at wheels of rope.

Not just rope but manila hemp, made from the fiber of the abaca, a.k.a. *Musa textilis,*
whose leafstalks

very much resemble those of the banana tree, though fruit is not what comes to mind,
given a room

with a small potbelly stove in the center encroached upon by columns of sea rigging
that reach up

to the anchors, several of which resemble meat hooks as they dangle from the ceiling
by the preservers.

Not just anchors, but the sacred anchor, and the screw anchor, and the stern anchor,
and the kedge,

as if being aboard a tug off Manhattan or a freighter in the South Pacific is both holy
and crude.

HENRY STREET

Head on, the facades of the tenements would expose little about each of the families
from the panes,
and a conventional lens wouldn't be able to include the worn-out block of buildings
all at once.
If the camera is moved to the end of the street the perspective is such that both sides
are pinched
into twin triangles of collective anonymity gradually receding to the far-off radiance
of skyscrapers,
triangles taking turns wearing the roof lines of each other in the morning or late sun
as in a game
two kids might play with a ball in the street if not for the treacherous footing caused
by old snow
like summer ocean surf washing up against what would be the sand if this were not
the gutter.

Old-Law Tenements: First Street

The houses that for years kept the facades of a row of old-law tenements from view
have been razed,
replaced by the foreman's office and wood scaffolding where excavation has begun
for a subway.
The seven dingy brick dwellings seem the same height, like the lower teeth of a man
who through life
has had a bad habit of grinding them together when he's been in a moment of worry
or boredom.
Two are as discolored as teeth long dead, but the others somehow shine awkwardly
in the direct sun
in spite of the slim pennants of laundry stretching out from many of the fire escapes
to the street poles,
in spite of the windows, some of which have been thoroughly cleaned and curtained
beside some broken.

Minetta Street, Nos. 2, 4, 6: 1935

Where once the trout stream called Minetta Brook worked its way through farmland
of Manhattan
until the beginning of the eighteenth century now stand three dreary brick buildings,
like immigrants
who, having lived long and difficult lives without ever learning the English language,
sit on a bench.
Two of them have elevated entrances with stone stairways and rickety black railings
used so much
the center of each step is as deeply eroded as a butcher-block table after two decades
with one butcher.
The difference is these buildings have been inhabited by everybody from ragpickers
to the old man
at the left negotiating stairs with the deliberation of somebody who knows next year
he must go too.

(All three buildings were demolished in 1936)

WEST STREET

As the photographer saw it, at an angle,
        focusing on the five tired brick buildings
partially obscured by a passing flatbed truck,
        highlighted by the sun at the end of the day.
A few bystanders at the bus stop to the left,
        a single gray skyscraper rising in the distance
of tiers and tiers of anonymous windows,
        mostly in shadow in spite of its height
because it's dusk, because it's a black-and-white,
        some ordinary images on emulsified paper.

Of art, Berenice Abbott said, "If a medium
        is representational by nature of the realistic
image formed by a lens, I see no reason
        why we should stand on our heads to distort
that function. On the contary, we should
        take hold of that very quality, make use of it,
and explore it to the fullest." Which means
        long before the arrival of the ground lens
we were light-sensitive creatures in search
        of borders to distinguish ourselves from others.

. . .

36

It's the viewfinder we were after all along,
        the little dark window to make the familiar
world miniature and mercifully out of context.
        When you get right down to it, all the soul wants
is a darkroom and a little free time to itself
        to sift through the infinity of glassine sleeves
filled with the negatives it's always promising
        to put in some logical order but never does,
though it remains hopeful it will use the tongs
        to lift the perfect version of itself out of the fixer.

III

Reckoning

THE SHORE

In memory of E. Clark Stillman

There's always a pause between ebb and flow.
      The ocean that's been reading to you is quiet,
as though a page has been torn from the book
      just as the narrative approaches the crisis point.
It has something to do with bluffs and dunes,
      the cosmic reordering of life based on the tides
pulling you in or away from the safety of shore.
      The calligraphy of seaweed on the page of sand

spells out nothing in particular but creates a tone
      as distinctive and mysterious as the moiré effect
of shallow water sliding across your bare feet.
      Once again the ocean has sent an internal memo
that the molecules read in a hurry and destroy.
      And yet there are other ways it makes contact,
such as the slowed-down Morse code of waves
      breaking over the rotting pylons of a ruined pier,

. . .

where at this moment everything seems placid,
        even those perched seagulls awaiting their signs.
It still feels that the harbingers are washing up,
        though on the other side of the island at high tide,
so that when you get there the sand is smooth,
        according to the ritual of giving and taking away.
On one hand, nature is vying for your attention,
        calling you over, putting its arm on your shoulder

as if about to whisper to you a well-kept secret,
        and you, yourself, wanting such, stare out to sea
with the hope and dread of someone in the past
        on the widow's walk watching for her husband.
Still, there is no message out where the shoals
        roil the dark water into an illegible, foamy script
so tantalizing since it is impossible to decipher
        the briny line that never says the same thing twice.

There is some consolation in the radiant sun
        so constant across your bare shoulders and back,
so thorough in its study of the grainy carpet
        over which you traverse in the throes of thought.

The mixture of sun and salt makes you feel
        that if you sat down in the right frame of mind
you could be turned into something as light
        and porous as a chip of balsa found in the sand.

And yet, how the sun always focuses on you
        as it does everybody else at one time or another,
not to dry you out as though you were a piece
        of papyrus on which it wished to write a letter,
a list of aspirations and failures for posterity
        after thinking long and hard about its double life,
but, rather, to work up the nerve to touch you,
        only to change its mind and make a gentle retreat.

You end where you begin, gazing with curiosity
        at the abandoned lighthouse at the edge of the jetty,
which appears to have an interpretation of the sea
        but keeps to itself now that it's been officially retired.
The gulls glide over the surface in slow motion
        as they do every afternoon in hungry reconnaissance
at an hour when the water is like wet newspaper,
        too far gone for someone to read, and the tide starts in.

Recreational

We're teed up in windbreakers on the familiar coast, shanking one ball after another into the sea
as if there is a lesson to be learned from watching a well-conceived idea go off-kilter and vanish.
We're mired in abject denial of the fact we have taken up weekend roller-blading on soft gravel
in front of the garage out back because we don't want neighbors to catch sight of us falling down.
Long ago, we might have driven down to the local trout stream to fish ourselves out of a funk,
hopefully on one of those forgotten weekday afternoons when the only car in the lot was our own.
Somewhere along the way all those endorphins that used to kick in after a few miles died off,
the body one day forsaking running uphill against the wind in the middle of winter to walk home.
Not that we aren't still capable of waiting patiently to get into a game of five-on-five on the corner,
it's only that we prefer shooting perfect jumpers by ourselves at the only backboard with no rim.

WESTERLY

If in the end happiness is something akin to sea grass
with its gift for leisure wafting on the back side of the dunes

behind a long, northern spit of beach closed due to erosion,
and sadness is at its keenest something like the repetition

of the everyday ambivalence of waves always eating at shore,
this might be cause for putting on shoes and heading inland.

On a sad day the sea air can tag along with you for miles
in silence, as if it were working up the nerve to say something wise,

or else to beg you to reconsider your strategic departure
just minutes before the sun begins to lose interest in the day,

but it never does, and by the time you get to the intersection
of the causeway and the road to the interior there are particulars

you didn't see when you were meandering in the other direction,
so that, except for the salt in your shirt the sea is all, but forgotten.
. . .

It takes a long time to figure out that being sad and being happy
are not in opposition to each other, as in high tides and low tides.

Despite what shrinks say, one does not beget the other either,
nor do they enter into some union for the rite of having any offspring.

What would it suggest about me if, when you asked me to state
the first thing that came into my mind when you said "west,"

I said "farther west"; what would it suggest about me
if, when you said "wrong," I said "more wrong" or "not so wrong"?

If I told you that night is nothing but an invisible colander
that every night slides over the sky so that stars are holes,

would you understand that I have come to treat metaphors
like beers cans tossed out by the side of the road I'm walking?

I have no way of knowing if the world changes its attitude
toward me as I make my way back whence I have wandered.

The trees look less harrowed, the grass looks less like burlap.
The venetian blinds in the window of a motel's stucco are still shut.

. . .

Part of me could take that as a sign somebody earlier closed the blinds
before turning down the covers to make love in the afternoon,

part of me could take that as a sign somebody's lying in despair,
the bourbon on the bedside table and blanket up to the chin,

part of me thinks both of the above at some point did happen,
maybe both on the same day before the troubled one got up and left.

WILD MOMENTUM

We have now arrived at a truism
so misunderstood it's a paradox.
The human machine was once very apt
at thinking big, for long stretches of time,
of the unimportant and meaningless,
as if it really mattered a great deal.
An ancient water poet studied the leaf
on the minor currents of a river,
before inking delicate ideograms
describing in detail every nuance.
He walked home by himself at dusk.

The river has darkened over the years,
otherwise our own eyes have darkened
from familiarity with the surface.
The water has turned more grainy with time
as if it were a Xerox of itself:
definition lost in reproduction.
We've also darkened and grown more brittle,
everything inside has become murky.

Yet things that matter to us do bob up
mysterious in the wild momentum
as if struggling in vain to right themselves.

It's enough to be glued to the railing
with so many others at lunch hour
toward the end of a millennium
that has grown unfamiliar to itself.
We're obstacles the wind accommodates
as it accommodates the skyscrapers
looming if we glance over the shoulder.
Sometimes it seems we fit into the scheme
so well we get a glimpse of the pattern
we desperately hope everything falls into
as we watch the water. Watch the water.

LOCOMOTIVE

Someone slips by you in the corridor of a crowded train, a stranger making his way
to the bar,
and for one unforgettable moment, you are pressed closer to the thick panel window
than is natural
because for the most part it is only children who press their small faces to clear glass
with wonder.
The arrival and departure of a river running under the tracks and a silhouetted farmer
on his tractor
are coupled in time like two consecutive freight cars in a train that stretches for miles
of prairie,
but while the water is almost immediately gone from sight, the farmer hovers silently
in the dusk,
until he's nothing more than a thought on the horizon as the locomotive surges ahead
toward the night.

Self Service

Somebody loves us all.
—Elizabeth Bishop

If only the culling of experience was as easy as pulling into a gas station and saying
Fill 'er up
to the man on duty, who lifts your camera off the dash while you are in the rest room
around back,
not because he is a thief, or even a shutterbug who has a collection of antique Leicas
in his house,
but because he has the spontaneous urge to hold the camera at arm's length and take
his portrait.
There is a kind of nonthreatening bewilderment that ambushes you a few days later
as you sit
in a docile armchair savoring the afterglow of reaching your destination by perusing
trip photos
only to come upon the unshaven face of a stranger in a grimy cap whose expression
is so neutral,
so unwilling to give you any clues about his background or motive that you can just
be thankful
he's not sitting across from you talking about schizophrenia while cleaning his nails
with a toothpick,
even though the inexplicable reason he spliced himself into your life does place you
in his debt.

ONE PART

Apart from the fretting, apart from the soon-to-be-lamented but as of now still-taken-for-granted,

apart from all the oversights and second guesses that go away only to call back later long distance

from a seaside resort in the winter of your memory, trying to urge you to reconsider your actions,

even though the suitcase is still in the closet and you have every intention of staying where you are.

Apart from the jokes and possibilities, apart from resolutions whispered at midnight years ago,

punch lines and promises long since torn from their moorings bobbing in the slatch of the mind.

Apart from misgivings and apprehensions heard but not heeded that have turned out to be true,

so that even the path you walk each night after work is ominous with the suggestion of the self,

solitude in the sound of a faraway cab coming to a stop on slush-covered pavement in the dark

followed by a momentous silence making you feel there is no doubt you are on loan from the past.

On Religion

As when you expect friends for lunch
              and they call you up to say traffic is bad,
they're running late, but everything's okay,
              they don't mind you starting without them.

Then there are the other irritants. Somebody
              must have died on his car horn somewhere
just far enough away from your window
              so that you only wonder if you hear it.

The ominous shadow passing overhead
              is vastly overrated, though there are moments
when you know precisely what time it is
              without checking your watch or dialing time.

The truth is prayers can develop leaks too,
              and it has nothing to do with how often
you do or don't use them, they just succumb
              a little while after the euphoria wears off.

PSALM

Most religions don't go out of fashion, they get sent back to the shop for lubrication
and new paint.
The priest trickling holy water on the infant's head imagines cutting unbiblical cords
of atheists
and the maharishi offering food and lodging at his geodesic dome wants to hand out
tin cymbals.
You did not have to be born at the same time as somebody else to know that a fatwa
is not food.
Because it's the finale of the millennium it does not mean there's not a stake out there
burning for you
as there is each year around this time even if you've done nothing worse than dream
of heresy.
It all comes down to questions of language, nothing a little "eth" at the end of a verb
won't fix.
Why else would the townspeople spend the better part of the day in church kneeling
on gravel?
Wouldn't it make sense to blow out the candles and hand the parishioners hyacinths
in ash urns?
If only it were common knowledge that not every beard who comes down the pike is
a magus.

54

NIGHT COMMUTE

This is the terminal-pride local,
        thin utopia for transient souls,
chauffeur for the supine memory.
        Bon soir, steel conductor, bearer
with your spine fed by live wires.
        I'm in you as you guide the night,

except you know nothing of night,
        nothing about time of day or locale
other than that blue idea in a wire
        giving a life to your one-way soul.
I am memorizing how you bear up
        under this routine without memory.

You have a destination, and memory,
        whether diamond day or coal night,
means little; the tracks give bearings
        so there's no need to study the locals
leaning out of hot windows like souls
        in an upper rung of Dante, high-wired,

. . .

or the dancer on the street, high wired,
        because he is half afraid of memory.
I have hair in front of me, and the soles
        of a man to the side sleeping off night,
stirring to take a swig when the local
        comes to a halt, to help him bear it all.

There's no dark wood. Trees are bare
        and unholy under the wiry light of cars.
The windows are silent, the locomotion
        full of slight lurches hardly memorable
to anyone familiar with this route at night.
        Confinement with others is so solitary.

But there's another kind of solitude
        in watching as the drunk is borne off
to a drowsy car or the scarf of night,
        the intricate city in the distance: wireless
circuitry in a laptop with its memory
        plagued by a virus that can't be located.

. . .

The last stop is memory, as bare
        and black as the entrance of a tunnel.
Wires dangle above like lost souls
        whose limbs keep remembering
where the local took them the nights
        they walked through the double doors.

SERIAL

Someone's changing channels in the next room,
thus music with intermittent static.

The ongoing process of indecision
by two elderly neighbors is automatic.

The stations have become service buddies
or children to be looked in on before bed.

At this hour very few words intrude,
the TV says *shhh* to itself again and again,

after the comic rhumba or detective fugue,
until just when the unsteady metronome

takes on greater significance, it ends.
The words aren't loud enough to make out,

but the tone of the script comes in clear:
Silence is the serial they most fear.

POST-ACHILLEAN

The campaign ends. Time makes its way
down side streets, an AWOL soldier.
Somewhere along the coast a gray turret
wakes up from a shallow doze and swivels
back toward the land.
                   But that is all,
the sea returns to its remedial reading of the sky,
the windows above the window boxes open.
Everything grows as quiet as a layer of coins
at the bottom of the fountain in a square.

The problem is we can never be sure
if there's someone out there on sentry duty.
We grew up being told somebody was on watch
though we never learned whose side he was on.
There's this part of us
                    that wants to salute,
which could lead to more rations and down time.
There's a part of us wanting to ream the rifle barrel.
We're more or less sitting on our helmets
with a convoy forever approaching in the distance.
. . .

Once in a while the permanently loose ends
of our lives gather around us to pay their respects
with varying degrees of sincerity, and we know
that soon they will board the flotilla of ships offshore
and drift heroically

                             out of sight to the next mission.
At which point the situation is alarmingly askew.
For instance, things aren't where they should be
according to the map, the sun remains fixed at noon,
and we have to press onward in search of our bearings.

STREET MUSIC

It has just started to rain and the macadam is coated with an invisible, viscous glaze
that's treacherous,
particularly when one of the woozy drivers heading uptown from the red-light zone
stops short
in order to ask directions to the final tavern or to let the passengers get a closer look
at a hiked skirt.
Dawn! What dawn is this one wades through like an anonymous tugboat in an eddy
of the river?
How long have the bells in the parapet of the dilapidated church been open-throated
and hammerless?
Night's rival is nothing more than a blank scroll of vellum parchment hiding the sky
from the city
as the first passenger buses make their servile way from street to street along a route
with no riders.

No one on the avenue is entirely sure of himself, though each has a knack for acting
determined,
at the wheel of the courier truck in the midday breeding ground of crosstown anger
for instance,
when heat rises from the yellow jackets with their meters running and engine hoods
slightly ajar

as a messenger on roller blades vanishes between two tractor trailers only to emerge unscathed,
half aware he's a survivor as he lowers himself to gather speed and raises his finger to the sky
because something about what he does is defiance, and something about it is beauty, determined
that morning by a phone call or fax or computer dot-matrix printout as well as a bit of danger.

There is no shade to speak of under the gaunt and withered trees along the sidewalk or in the park,
where a woman reclining on a folding chair holds a cardboard mirror under her chin much in vain.
The sky is so crowded with clouds it resembles cotton in the top of an aspirin bottle just opened
either by an infant whose parents are in the next room arguing or an elderly woman with a migraine.
Even the plastic plants on the fire escape above the sooty awning of the delicatessen look fatigued
near two gray pigeons side by side in a jerry-rigged nest on top of an air conditioner in indifference,
as though they've been staring at the same collection of parked cars and storefronts for decades.
. . .

At certain hours of the day the incinerator chimney atop a high-rise across the street belches smoke,

which has a way of hovering against the backdrop of white sky with the irreverence of an idler

from the last century dressed in a shabby cape who looks about and doesn't believe his ash eyes

how much of the river is now obscured by tiers of plain buildings made out of glass and steel.

When the wind is headed right the smoke drifts to the edge of the roof, as if the idler wants to see

a long, slim line of traffic below stretching out in both directions like an oily necktie and how far

we have come from the contradiction of parasols and horse dung before he vanishes into the air.

Gradually they grow accustomed to the oddity of lining up in front of a cement wall to draw cash

from a machine that might take several minutes to mull over an order before ejecting a few bills,

but they don't feel comfortable with a camera's soap-bubble blue lens aimed at them from above,

because although they're told it is for protection they don't like being photographed in this setting.

They have no choice but to cross their fingers that the check they deposited recently has cleared,

and that the machine doesn't malfunction and reach a decision to give out no money
or eat the card,
meaning they will have to pass up an evening of Chinese takeout and a video rental
and walk home.

We are linked, you know. Not necessarily like the fifteen kindergarten kids walking
in single file,
all tied together in canvas vests of a yellow so intense they appear mildly radioactive
in certain light
as cheerfully they snake their way through the midmorning crosscurrents of people to
a playground.
Not necessarily like the man on the street who pretends he is talking to the President of
"this fuckhole"
via a phone receiver with a severed wire that wraps around his neck once and hangs
down his chest,
but by the exaggerated gestures he makes with his free hand suggesting he is aware
of his audience,
especially the ones who look up at him with a peculiar mixture of wonder and terror
as they're led by.

With phlegm-colored hair combed down in careless haste atop his face recrudescent
from a half pint
of bourbon, the top of which sticks out of the right back pocket where often a wallet
might protrude,

and an underweight body so tall and always slightly tilted forward it should tip over
with each step
taken toward vehicles lining up at the stoplight again and again throughout the day,
he looks pitiful,
so pitiful that by the evening he has enough coins to buy another bottle and stumble
into the subway,
where a pasty-skinned man sitting on a piece of carpet lining strums a guitar quietly
for loose change
until the first one nudges the open guitar case with his foot and yells at the musician
to quit begging.

Tonight somebody wants to cut flesh on the jagged outcroppings of corrugated steel
on the avenue,
somebody wants to bound down to the rank gutter along the subway tracks to touch
the third rail.
O city of knee-deep potholes and manhole covers spewing maniac demons of steam
in the streets,
city of gypsy rats and cabs rummaging about after midnight with the rabid insomnia
of base instinct,
O city of the overabundance of perpendicular angles, where verticals and horizontals
dice the air.
Tonight the major constellation is an acetylene blue star, which bursts into an infinity
of white sparks
every time the chop-shop workman touches the fender bolts or engine block mounts
of a hot car.

TRANSIT AUTHORITY

The journey is never what's expected.
      But we persist. Something goes wrong
on the other side of the tattered freeway
      so that traffic is backed up for miles.
Someone gets out of his car to stare ahead
      with a hand shielding his eyes from the sun
the way the sailors once did sighting land,
      only his frown hints he may be on empty.

Minutes from now he could be scrambling
      through an opening in the hurricane fence
or walking with a can down the on-ramp
      where some drivers now escape in reverse.
We're lucky the road spreads out before us
      like a clear runway, but we're not satisfied.
It's as if the odometer is stuck on the nines,
      the infernal ticking of the last digit won't stop.

Gradually, the familiar skyline looms ahead,
      gently coated with the smoggy haze of dusk,
in sharp contrast to the assortment of cars
      that have been picked to the bone and burned

appearing periodically in the breakdown lane,

       like profane doodles in the margin of a Bible

you just happen to pick up in a motel room,

       the ones that smudge if you try to erase them.

Were we meant to travel at such speed?

       Is it only a sensation that things pass us by,

as if televised, as if programmed for us,

       a myriad of facades inevitably giving way

to sudden vistas where we get a glimpse

       of the industrial water gleaming in the distance,

soon to be interrupted by a row of windows,

       some containing figures we can't quite make out?

Experience turns into a handful of change

       dropped again and again into the metal basket

so that the gate goes up and we move on,

       well aware that at this juncture the road narrows

and we become part of the same intensity

       others feel, even when they roll up their windows

and proceed with the tentative resolve

       of angels approaching earth for the first time.

RECKONING

I

Lock and load. That's what the finch thinks. Honest
renderings have gone out of fashion, brushes
dropped in the turp. Honest. The sun is armed
and unavailable for comment now.
Maybe we should go have an espresso
until we get the proper shade of light,
as if talking about things will bring them
out in the open like good biscotti.
Did light ever affect us the way bombs
asleep in distant silos do, or don't?
You get the feeling that the big fella
has set up his easel in a meadow,
not so much to capture the flight of birds
as to let the stretched canvas lie in state.

II

Yet letting the stretched canvas lie in state
conjures up images of the public
in one of those collective-fugue mindsets
as each peers in the casket at what is
already on his mind in the first place.
We know even distant friends best when they're
finally beyond our recognition.
Better to be reduced to a handful
of ashes poured out of a leather pouch
from the back of a slow-moving vessel
whose passengers are no more than strangers.
It does not take long for the roiling wake
to draw even the most averted eyes
to see what instantly becomes the sea.

III

To see what instantly becomes the sea
is not always a seminal moment.
After all, where does grand vision come from?

From leaning out too far over the rail?
The one time you have not brought a slicker,
angels arrive laterally like a squall.
All that matters is the degree of black
coordinated at random by virtue
of who is in eyeshot at the moment.
The best mood change may be you walking out
of a church funeral into sunlight
with a crowd none of whom you know at all.
Some say if you really liked the deceased,
you won't have any urge to go back in.

IV

You don't have any urge to go back in?
Too many rows of red-glass candle cups
suggest too much saintly order. Those pews.
So many kneeling, still not enough seats.
Nota: the sacrament is a product
shipped in bulk from somewhere in the Midwest.
Under the apse, in the basement, boxes
of wafers and wax line the walls like food
in a bomb shelter stocked to outlast God.

Be thankful there are others who believe
in the musical chairs of religion;
each sitteth at the right hand of the aisle
or the left, all but one of them secure
without the notion they are ground zero.

V

Without the notion they are ground zero,
aware the tavern won't open till noon,
Laurel and Hardy visit a psychic
who gives the thumbs down to their clammy palms.
"The future is just history's entrails"
is what the woman says for fifteen bucks,
three crumpled fives she stuffs toward a crotch
hidden under her own ample stomach.
Back out in the now ominous bright light,
Stan wrinkles his brow and plays with his tie
for comfort like a kid with a bedsheet.
Ollie snaps his suspenders and looks up
at the sky, as if it could show some sign
encoded or cryptic, and says, "Let's eat."

VI

Encoded, cryptic, the saying "Let's eat"
out of the mouth of a trench-coated spy
might mean there's a microchip in the blintz
or poison in the noodles Romanoff
secretly touted as the day's special.
But even cold warriors wax nostalgic,
and the gray uneasiness disperses
like a mixture of rain and pesticide
seeping into the remote aquifers
waiting to inflect the flavor of crops.
Round tables are for facing each other
over fortifying bowls of corn soup
from a recipe handed down from God.
Notice that no one offers to say grace.

VII

Notice that no one offered to say grace
for the meal. There were more familiar songs
in the guests' minds because of chardonnay.

Everybody knew but dared not tell
why the evening resembled candle wax
pooling slowly at the base of the shafts.
Somebody should have popped somebody else
on the kisser, somebody should have leapt
from the dining room window full of stars,
though *that* would have disrupted the dessert
of apples, pears, grapes, and a spread of Brie,
Reblochon, Pont l'Évêque, *vacherin*, *Comté*,
Camembert, Chavignol, *bleu de Salers*,
all neatly arranged around an ash urn.

VIII

All neatly arranged around an ash urn,
the children in the museum listen
to the scholar explain in simple terms
the ritual of death as sacrifice.
It is not the artist but the crude kill
that comes to life out of an ancient dye
so surprisingly vivid under glass.

The class keeps inching forward as if drawn
to a schoolyard injury or fight
where the presence of blood on the pavement
drains the color out of everything else
until someone comes to hose down the scene.
The kids are too young to ask the scholar
why there's no mention of beauty or truth.

IX

There is no mention of beauty or truth,
in truth, because everyone's still sleeping
after a night of philosophers and wine.
The branches are hospitable to birds
that keep vigil without passing judgment.
Silence coats the street in both directions
except for the occasional taxi
whirring by in search of its first fare.
Even the oven in the bakery
around the corner is cool for one day.
Soon there'll be others around to advance
ideas, but for the moment the windows
are in charge, especially the dark ones
at the end of the street that never open.

X

Beware of windows that never open.
The frames have been painted too many times,
often different colors, so that if chipped
they show the history of landlord taste.
Or else rain has somehow seeped in the cracks,
swelling the wood so it cannot slide.
Be extra careful if the shades are down.
Beware of windows that are open, too.
Infants can crawl out of them and fall.
People can be heard having arguments
so late at night the neighbors start shouting
epithets that always sound more vulgar
in the dark. Keep an eye out for someone
waiting for you to undress. Then do it.

XI

Waited a minute to undress. Then did,
and when completely naked stared across
the alley at the one who held himself
without expression. Felt oddly aroused
to have control over need and pleasure,

his and mine, and for a moment lost
track of the distance between us and touched
and touched again until something remote
inside the mind drifted into focus,
nothing to do with ecstasy or shame,
a sense of the world being so barren,
so meaningless at times I should step away
from the authority of my window,
and when I saw myself clearly, he came.

XII

And when they saw themselves clearly, they came
to new conclusions, the shelf life of jokes,
for example, was not what it once was.
They now had very little in common.
Laurel's penchant for pantomime dwindled
so much he simply wanted to retire
to the country where he could be serious
about flowers. Hardy entertained thoughts
of signing on with the Foreign Legion,
though in his heart he knew he would end up
passing afternoons of coffee and pie,

silverware and salt-and-pepper shakers
laid out on the table before him
in countless military formations.

XIII

How countless military formations
insinuate their way into mainstream lives:
the navy tuck, for example, imposed
to crease and clutch the corners of a bed,
be it the bed of lovers or the dead.
It's the renaissance of boots and fatigues
holed up in the cold for the duration,
or warm mornings on a campus corner.
The use of middle fingers to salute
has also arrived, not just on the fringe.
The custom of folding the flag three ways
so as to form a perfect triangle
has been preserved so that the general
can march out to surrender in a field.

XIV

Anyone walking alone in a field
might happen upon a wood skeleton,
the still-upright remnants of an easel
with a blown-down canvas nearby, sharp stalks
sticking up through the time-slackened center.
Anyone might pick up the blank canvas
and, out of a sense of order, or pity,
set it back on the stand. It wouldn't matter
if, so decayed, the fabric might peel off
the frame and hang down like papery skin.
Could the one great artist we'll never know
walk out one morning to paint a landscape,
take stock of things, and lose inspiration?
Lock and load. That's what the finch thinks. Honest.